MY BEST FRIEND

Tamsin Oglesby

MY BEST FRIEND

OBERON BOOKS
LONDON
WWW.OBERONBOOKS.COM

First published in 2000 by Faber and Faber Ltd

This edition published in 2011 by Oberon Books Ltd
521 Caledonian Road, London N7 9RH
Tel: 020 7607 3637 / Fax: 020 7607 3629
e-mail: info@oberonbooks.com
www.oberonbooks.com

A catalogue record for this book is available from the British
Library.

PB ISBN: 978-1-84943-060-9
E ISBN: 978-1-78319-241-0

Cover image by James Illman

Visit www.oberonbooks.com to read more about all our books
and to buy them. You will also find features, author interviews and
news of any author events, and you can sign up for e-newsletters
so that you're always first to hear about our new releases.

Characters

EM

BEE

CHRIS

My Best Friend was first performed at The Hampstead Theatre on the 20th January 2000 with the following cast:

EM – Teresa Banham

BEE – Eve Matheson

CHRIS – Sara Crowe

Creatives

Director – Anthony Clark

Designer – Patrick Connellan

Lighting Designer – Tim Mitchell

Sound Designer – Dean Whiskens

Fight Director – Terry King

Choreographer – Francesca Jaynes

ACT ONE

A rustic French farmhouse, part of which has been tastefully developed, other parts of which are in a state of disrepair. The verandah is separated from the main interior by large windows, which are, at the moment, open.

It is a warm evening. Two women in their thirties, EM and BEE, sit outside, with coffee and tea on the table before them. EM is English, BEE is Irish. BEE's eyes are closed. EM is deep in thought.

EM: So, if the clocks go forward then…what?

BEE: No, they're going back.

EM: Back?

BEE: We gain an hour.

EM: Back. No, that can't be right.

BEE: Yes we gain – sure it is – it's, what, nine o'clock now – this time tomorrow it'll be eight o'clock.

EM: So, but hang on. Then you're an hour behind.

BEE: Yes.

EM: So you've lost an hour.

BEE: No, no, listen now. You're an hour behind, so you've gained – think about it – you'll have an extra hour in the day, won't you?

EM: Right. Of course. Yes. So if you went to bed earlier…then you'd wake up at the same time.

BEE: As what?

EM: As today.

BEE: What?

EM: Oh, let's start again. Okay, we go to bed at twelve, say, and we put, no let's say we don't put our clocks back, and we wake up at eight, new time, but it is in fact, according to our clocks, it'll say nine, won't it?

BEE: Eight new time, nine old time, yeah.

EM: Oh my god.

BEE: What?

EM: I can't remember the last time I got up at nine o'clock.

BEE: No but it won't be, will it? It won't actually be nine o'clock. Because the thing is, if you usually wake up at eight then you'll wake up – if you go to bed at twelve – you'll still only wake up at eight, if you don't change your watch, that is, and if you do it'll be seven, GMT, which is great because you'll have slept for the same amount of time but you'll be an hour ahead...

EM: But I want to wake up at nine. I don't want to wake up at seven.

BEE: Em.

EM: I want to wake up and see nine o'clock, and roll over onto my freshly baked croissant. And I don't usually wake up at eight anyway. In fact I never wake up at eight.

BEE: Well when do you usually wake up?

EM: Six.

BEE: Well there you are then, Elsie Marley. Seven, eight or nine. Whatever happens you'll be having a lie in. But you know what?

EM: What?

BEE: France is an hour ahead.

EM: Oh no.

BEE: Which means…

EM: Pish.

BEE: Which means you lose one, you gain one, you're quits.

EM: Nothing happens.

BEE: Or everything happens. But in a vortex.

EM: Oh these stupid hours, flying around the place. As long as I get my eight hours sleep I don't care whether the world is going forwards or backwards to be frank.

BEE helps herself to coffee and offers EM the teapot.

BEE: How's the tea?

EM: Fine. *(She refuses more.)* How's the coffee?

BEE: Shite. I'd like a cigarette now.

EM: No you wouldn't.

BEE: No I wouldn't. *I would not like a cigarette.* Stick a packet of the little bastards in front of me there, I'd tear em up and throw them over the balcony to their death. Jesus, that's /some drop he's got there.

EM points excitedly up into the sky.

EM: There, there, there, look! Shooting star. /Look, look!

BEE: Where? Where?

EM: There! You missed it.

BEE: I've never not seen so many shooting stars.

EM: How could you miss it again? /It was right there!

BEE: Withdrawal symptoms. Can't concentrate on anything beyond here.

EM: Three in one night. Isn't that amazing?

BEE: Yeah. No, sad actually. Three dying meteors.

EM: Oh don't.

BEE: That's what they are. Dying meteors. Size of that moon, though. Is it not the most delicious moon you ever saw? It's like a gorgeous great scoop of nougat ice cream.

EM: Stop it, I'm hungry.

BEE: I'm starving. I knew we ought to have stopped on the way.

EM: I was sure there'd be something here. An old tin of olives, bit of garlic, you know.

BEE: Will I go and explore, have a little drive, see what there is?

EM: No, don't worry, /nothing'll be open this time of night.

BEE: I don't mind. I could just hop in the car –

EM: No, it's okay. You drink your shite coffee and I'll drink my tea.

BEE starts to sing melodramatically, in imitation of Hazel O' Conor.

BEE: And we're… sitting here… playing so cool, thinking… what will be will be.

EM joins in.

EM: I move a little closer to you…

BEE: Not knowing quite what to do and I – /I'm feeling all fingers and thumbs –

EM: I'm feeling all fingers and thumbs…I spill my tea…oh silly me. /I move – wonder will you stay now…stay now…stay now…stay now…stay now

BEE: And I wonder will you stay now…stay now…stay now… stay now…or will you just politely /say 'goodnight'

EM: – say 'goodbye'.

BEE: This moment I've been waiting for…is it something you've been waiting for…waiting for too?

They laugh.

BEE: Good old Hazel.

EM: I told Cob, listen, I told Cob the other day that I've been having an affair.

BEE: What?

EM: I said, I tried to find the best moment to break it to him, but in the end I couldn't wait til I had his attention I just blurted it out when he was in the middle of shaving and he just went 'hmmmm?' you know, absent-minded, so I sat him down on the loo seat and said 'I'm having an affair.' And then he looked at me with this incredible expression, like he knew me but couldn't quite place me, then he fuzzed over again and said – do you know what he said?

BEE: Jesus Em.

EM: No, he said, 'Don't be silly, Em.' Don't be silly. Like he was telling Louis off for burping at the dinner table and that really made me mad. That's all I was going to say, but then I couldn't stop, I went on and on about how this guy had just pursued me and pursued me and eventually I gave in, and then suddenly he looked so small and hurt I started crying and then he started crying it was awful I wished I'd never said it.

Pause.

BEE: My god, Emma. Who is he?

EM: Who?

BEE: The affair. /Who is this person?

EM: I'm not having an affair.

Pause.

BEE: You're not?

EM: I'm not – *NO* – I said – of course I'm not – I just wanted to see what would happen.

BEE: What would happen?

EM: If I said I was having an affair.

BEE: Why?

EM: I don't know.

BEE *(Softly.)* Christ.

EM: What?

BEE: Sometimes I wonder whether I know you at all.

EM: That's what he said.

BEE: I mean, if you want to have an affair –

EM: I don't want to have an affair. It's just all my friends are breaking up, and it's unnerving, you know. A few years ago it was all weddings, now they're all getting divorced. *(Pause.)* What? If I want to have an affair, what?

BEE: How can you say that? Lil's just got married.

EM: Well, alright, Lil, yes, /okay, I'll give you Lil.

BEE: Helen and Nick, they're still together.

EM: Not married though.

BEE: Happily living together. /Alex and Martina.

EM: Everyone else is getting divorced.

BEE: Bollocks they are. Some of them are happily single, some of them are gay, some of them are workaholics, some of them are –

EM: One parent families.

BEE: One parent families, some of them are abroad, some of them are dead.

EM: Who's dead?

BEE: No one. Tina Elton?

EM: Bee.

BEE: Anyway, what are you talking about? You're happily married, for god's sake.

EM: I know I know I know.

BEE: Well behave yourself.

EM: I am. I am.

Pause. BEE stares at EM, shakes her head in disbelief.

EM: So, Adam. You've not actually told me what happened yet. I mean, why, I mean how you're feeling, you know, about Adam. Are you alright?

Long silence.

EM: /I'm sorry, if you don't want –

BEE: I have a friend called Aidan, really tall, strong, but so gentle, you know, like the giant in the fairy stories –

EM: I know, yes, I've met him, /he's lovely –

BEE: Well, he's just come back from one of those safaris
in Zimbabwe. It was fantastic and all that, but one day
he went up this mountain on his own, just him and his
map and a bottle of water (and probably a packet of
fags, knowing him) and he sets off in the direction of this
waterfall, but nothing is where it should be. First of all he
thinks it's him. The map indicates a ravine, say, and all he
can see is a little dip in the ground. So he carries on a part
of the way like that, imagining things to be there which
clearly aren't there, until he realises the map is crap and he
decides instead to follow the sun, right, good old boy scout
that he is. But he has this terrible feeling with every step
that he's going further and further in the wrong direction.
And then he starts to panic because his sun is beginning to
set – okay – the sun is going down, and with the sun, the
heat. So now he's cold and hungry and lost as childhood.
/But he manages to find a cave just before night

EM: Scary.

BEE: falls, and he spends the coldest, loneliest night of his life
curled up in it like a little cub. Next morning, sun comes
up, he retraces his steps, climbs down the mountain, no
problem. It's only when he gets back home he figures it
out. He's flicking through some travel magazine and there
it is. Zimbabwe, of course, is in the southern hemisphere.
And there he was, following the sun, like it was in the
northern hemisphere, so everything was, in fact, upside
down. His instincts were screaming 'wrong way' all along,
but he ignored them because his logic was screaming 'right
way' even louder. And he felt such a fool. A total bloody
eejit.

*Silence. EM is unsure, at first, whether BEE has finished. She
laughs.*

EM: Of course. You'd never think of that, would you? I
certainly wouldn't, anyway. How funny. *(Pause.)* So this
guy, Aidan. Is he are you –

BEE: So that's how I'm feeling.

EM: Sorry?

BEE: About Adam.

Pause.

BEE: You asked me how I'm feeling. That's how I'm feeling. A total bloody eejit.

EM: Oh Bee.

BEE: I was going by the wrong sun.

EM: I'm so sorry.

BEE: Should have noticed months, years ago. Do you know, when he left he said 'I love you, Bee'. Can you imagine? All those years and he chooses to say 'I love you' when it's over.

EM: Scared of emotion.

BEE: No, just lazy. He never did anything he didn't have to do.

EM: Yeah, you're right. I always thought he was quite lazy.

BEE: A typical economist. Always saving things, himself, the truth. What do you mean?

EM: I mean he wasn't – nothing – I just mean he was quite, he could be quite unforthcoming sometimes. You know, like you say, just lazy, probably.

BEE: Unforthcoming? You think he was unforthcoming?

EM: Well, yes. Maybe that's the wrong word, but it took quite a lot to get him out of himself sometimes, you know.

BEE: You think so? You've never said that before.

EM: It's not a criticism, /I just – it's just an observation.

BEE: No, it's interesting. What you think, what people think. I didn't know you thought that about him because you never really know, and some people have said things which frankly amaze me, have amazed me. Andrea, the other day, she said she'd never really trusted him and she always thought he had his eye on the main chance. Whatever that means. And my friend, Faith, said 'yeah, I always thought he was a bit sly.' I mean, for god's sake, you know, what does that make me? Do they think it makes me feel better? No, it makes me feel like I've been waddling about with my head in the sand and my arse in the air all this time. Jesus. And these are my friends. What they must think of me. *(Pause.)* You don't think that do you?

EM: Of course I don't. I was just trying – I liked him, you know that. *(Silence.)* So, the thing about children…?

BEE: Yeah, he was never going to change his mind. I guess I should at least give him credit for consistency there.

EM: Oh god, I wish there was something I could do.

BEE: There is and you're doing it. It's great to be here.

BEE stands, meanders to the edge of the verandah, looks over the edge, tests it with her foot.

Do you know, apart from my parents, I've known you longer than anyone else in my life?

EM: Yup. Thirty something years.

BEE: Boyfriends. They come and go. But here we are, and I can tell you anything. With Adam, I'd need an appointment to talk about *us,* you know, and even then I'd have to get him drunk.

CHRIS appears in the doorway of the house. She carries a hold-all. She is the same age as BEE and EM, more made-up and dressed up.

Blackout as CHRIS speaks.

CHRIS: /Hello? Ooooh.

BEE: Oh not again.

EM: Oh No.

BEE: It's like living in the third world. No, I'll get it.

EM makes for the fuse box but BEE is up and heading towards it instead. CHRIS enters the room.

CHRIS: /Em!

EM: Sometimes they do just go whoosh and come straight back on on their own. What?

BEE: Is it the one on the left?

EM: Right. Why did you say 'Em'?

BEE: I didn't.

Lights. BEE and EM jump out of their skins on seeing CHRIS.

CHRIS: Oh thank god it's you darling/

EM: Chris! What on earth –

CHRIS: Thought I'd got the wrong house, taxi's gone disaster. Although frankly, quite frankly, I'd rather play murder in the dark with machete than get back in the car with that horrid little Frenchman. I've just had the most ghastly journey with this man. You know what I'm like, always choose the duffers – trust me – I sail straight past a queue of gorgeous pouting frogs and get into the cab of a toad. God I'm exhausted. All the way from Avignon he leered at me and then he seemed to think – when he asked me what I did and I said 'research' – he seemed to think I'd be up for a shag in the back of his car! God knows what I said, obviously means complete fucking tart in French. So he stopped in the middle of nowhere – for a slash, he said, 'pour faire aggrandir l'herbe', you know, and he disappeared for bloody ages, obviously expecting me to follow him, if you please, so I sat there thinking, 'nobody knows I'm here, oh my god, I'm going to die and become a statistic' and then eventually he emerges from the shrub ostentatiously wiping his hands, like this, wiping the spunk off his hands, you know, *disgusting,* dirty great smirk on his face, and then he gets in the car and he doesn't stop talking.

EM: Chris. /What are you doing here?

CHRIS: All the way here, gabbing away like radio Luxembourg and every time he stops at a light he puts his hand on my knee – made me sit in the front, I don't know, maybe that's what taxi drivers do in France, I thought, bloody pervert, let me out of here. I feel completely and utterly invaded I can tell you.

EM: Did you take his number? You should report him.

CHRIS: No, happens to me all the time. *(She strides about the verandah.)* Well this is alright, isn't it? I like the red. Very distressed-chic. It's a sort of barn, isn't it really?

EM: Chris. What on earth are you doing here?

CHRIS: Well, it's an extraordinary coincidence really – *(She breaks off, as if noticing BEE for the first time.)* – hello, sorry, I'm – *(She stops, taking her in properly now.)* Oh my god. It's not. Oh my god. Bee Hannon. Do you know, I was thinking only the other day I was thinking, I probably wouldn't recognise her if I sat on her. But here you are. Bee Hannon. My god. And what's amazing, do you know, you haven't changed. Even your hair is the same. Have you had it cut? I mean obviously you've had your hair cut in what, sixteen, eighteen years, whatever it is, I mean *changed* really. Or has it always been the same? Style, that is.

EM: Chris –

BEE: Why do you keep calling her Chris?

CHRIS: It's my name. *(Pause.)* Oh, because of Tina, you mean. No, I haven't called myself Tina for years. Christina. I just use the front bit now. Such a surprise, my god, he didn't say you'd be here as well.

BEE: Who didn't?

CHRIS: No, what happened is I rang up and Cob told me where you were and I said 'oh, I'm going to France', so he gave me your address only he didn't say it was outside the village which is why I've been going round and round the bloody piazza thing with this pervert. I'm exhausted. You wouldn't have an old glass of wine hanging about there would you? I think I might give way at the knees in a minute.

EM: Haven't got any, I'm afraid. We just arrived today.

CHRIS: No wine? But this is France!

EM: And I'm on the wagon anyway. There's still some tea in the pot.

CHRIS: On the wagon? /What reason have you –

EM: If I'd known you were coming, obviously I'd have got supplies, you know.

CHRIS: What I'll do, he's gone now hasn't he, but what I'll have to do, I'll nip up the road to the village and pick up a bottle or two. Me and Bee'll make up for you, won't we? Oh, it is good to see you. Both of you!

She embraces EM and stops just short of embracing BEE.

CHRIS: *(To BEE.)* You look really well. Doesn't she, look really well? Such a surprise to see you here! *(To EM.)* Oh, and last week – all these coincidences – you'll never guess who I bumped into last week sent his love to you. Guess, go on, guess.

EM: I don't know.

CHRIS: Extra Maths. Sat at the back. Huge.

EM: You know I can never remember these things.

CHRIS: Walked like this. *(She rolls from side to side.)*

EM: Oh, not – what's his name?

CHRIS: Like a penguin.

EM: I know, I know –

CHRIS: *(In a high voice.)* With a high voice, do you remember? Huge body and this little squeaky voice at the top of it.

EM: Don't tell me, don't tell me.

CHRIS: Lardy Hardy.

EM: Lardy Hardy, that's it!

CHRIS: Lardy Hardy. Can you believe it? There he was in the middle of this function. Still got an arse the size of England, but he was with this woman I know vaguely and god it was embarrassing because he remembered my name, (only it was my old one so we had all that) and so she said, 'oh, you know each other' and I looked at him and thought, 'yes, but I have no idea what your *name* is', I mean 'Lardy

Hardy', I couldn't very well call him that, could I? What was his bloody name?

EM: Don't ask me.

CHRIS: Well it was you he fancied.

EM: Martin?

CHRIS: No, not Martin. Began with M though, I think. Mike?

EM: Mark!

BEE: Duncan Hardy.

CHRIS: /Of course, Duncan.

EM: Duncan, that's it, Duncan. Why did we call him Lardy anyway?

CHRIS: You remember, he used to skive off to the coffee pot every lunch break and stuff himself with lardy cake.

EM: Yeuch, disgusting. Makes me feel sick just thinking of it.

(EM notices that BEE isn't really joining in.) You alright, Bee?

BEE: Fine.

She strides over to CHRIS and smacks her hard across the face. CHRIS reels backwards, then re-establishes her position as though it never happened. Pause.

BEE: You smoke?

CHRIS: Yes.

BEE: Can I have one?

Silence. They set back to:

CHRIS: What was his bloody name?

EM: Don't ask me.

CHRIS: Well it was you he fancied.

EM: Martin?

CHRIS: No, not Martin. Began with M though, I think. Mike?

EM: Mark!

BEE: Duncan Hardy.

CHRIS: /Of course, Duncan.

EM: Duncan, that's it. Duncan. Why did we call him Lardy anyway?

CHRIS: You remember, he used to skive off to the coffee pot every lunch break and stuff himself with lardy cake.

EM: Yeuch, disgusting. Makes me sick just to think of it.

(EM notices that BEE isn't really joining in.) You alright, Bee?

BEE: Fine. *(She walks over to CHRIS and confronts her. Pause.)* You smoke?

CHRIS: Yes.

BEE: Can I have one?

EM: /No.

CHRIS: Sure.

EM: Bee, what are you doing?

BEE: Tomorrow. I'll stop tomorrow.

CHRIS: Not you as well. Is it Lent or something?

BEE: I will.

EM: Bee!

CHRIS offers BEE a cigarette. BEE takes it.

BEE: Thanks.

EM: Give it back, give it back!

BEE: You can have a drink, /I don't mind.

EM: That's not the point. I don't want a drink.

BEE: It's just a fag.

EM: It's not just a fag. It's a *breach of trust*.

CHRIS: Whoops. I've walked into a war zone.

BEE: Breach of trust.

EM: Yes – Bee! If you smoke that thing...

CHRIS: Oh the age of giving up. I gave up once and my sense of smell came back it was disgusting. The world stinks of old fish. And all that bollocks about living longer. You add up all the time you waste thinking about giving up, then giving up, then evangelising about it afterwards, add it all up, that's your net, then take it away from your gross, the gross amount of years lived, you end up with the same as you would if you'd never bothered giving up only more miserable.

Pause. BEE gives the cigarette back. Silence.

EM: So where are you staying for goodness' sake?

CHRIS: Place called Orgon near Avignon with my cousin, Jean-Paul, sweet sweet man, we're very, you know, /he's always had a bit of a – what?

BEE: How long, how long are you staying there?

CHRIS: What?

BEE: How long are you staying? There?

CHRIS: Oh I don't know. Ça depends. How about you guys?

EM: A week. A whole week without putting on a nappy or brushing anyone's teeth. /Bliss.

CHRIS: /Except your own, I hope.

BEE: Although it's not really a holiday, is it? What it is, we're helping to do the place up, that's why we're here, awful lot of work to do, I can't tell you. A friend of Em's bought it recently, hasn't had the time, you know, so.

CHRIS: Hence the lack of front door.

BEE: Exactly, no front door.

CHRIS: And this here. *(She indicates the edge of the verandah.)* Fffhoo, that's one hell of a drop.

BEE: Have to put a bar – balcony – balustrade up there, soon as we get a minute.

CHRIS: Jolly little place. Bit spartan. But nice.

EM: There's a swimming pool round the back.

CHRIS: /A pool!

BEE: Freezing though. Unheated. Anyway, we probably won't have time for that, will we. Oh my god, when did we say we'd have to be getting up tomorrow morning? Seven? Six? I'm shattered already, I think I should be off to bed.

EM: Bee. It's not ten o'clock yet.

BEE: Yes but we lost an hour, didn't we? On the way over. I think that's why I'm so, you know.

EM: Yes, but we're going to gain another one in a minute, aren't we. You can't go to bed yet.

BEE: No, but it's not until two in the morning they go back, and I'm tired now.

EM: Two?

BEE: Yes.

(Pause.)

EM: So if you went to bed at two –

BEE: Oh don't start that again, please. Anyway, there's no question of my going to bed at two.

EM: No, okay, alright. But I think what you need is food anyway, not sleep.

CHRIS: I've got a baguette and some cheese here if you want. Never leave the house without them.

EM: Fantastic. Yes please.

CHRIS goes to find them in her bag.

CHRIS: She's a bit anorexic, his wife, you know, forgets mealtimes altogether, so I always need something to keep me going. /Doesn't

EM: Who did you say you were staying with?

CHRIS: stop her thrusting food at me the rest of the day though. My cousin, you know, Jean-Paul. He's a darling. He's always had a bit of a crush on me, actually, but, you know, there's no need, I mean we get on really well, it's just his wife, Celine, she keeps on, we can't be alone for one minute without her bursting in on us with baskets of freshly picked grapes or olives or some god-forsaken vegetable. She's a nightmare. I'm dying for a pee, actually. Where's the pissoir?

She puts the bread and cheese on the table.

EM: Through there, left. It's just a hole, I'm afraid.

CHRIS: Aren't we all, darling.

EM laughs. BEE doesn't. CHRIS goes. BEE looks frantically at EM.

BEE: Oh god. What am I going – I'm going to say something.

EM: You can say what you like.

BEE: No I can't. What am I going to do?

EM: Just be /normal.

EM starts laying plates etc. for the food. She eats as she does so.

BEE: Can you hear my heart? It's so loud. Oh god, it hurts. Is she going to stay? She can't stay.

EM: She'll have to now. /Just for the night.

BEE: No, there's no room.

EM: Bee, come on. You haven't seen her for years.

BEE: Exactly.

EM: She's changed. You've changed. We all have.

BEE: Don't you dare.

EM: What?

Pause.

BEE: Just passing through is she? In France? On her way to the boulangerie?

EM: So it seems. What? *(Pause.)* What?

BEE: After eighteen years. Christ.

EM: It's not – I've seen her. I see her, don't I? We keep in touch.

BEE: Why?

EM: Bee!

BEE: No, why?

EM: What kind of a question is that?

BEE: Why do you still see her? How can you still see her?

EM: I've known her for years. She's one of my oldest friends, like you. /Just because – *(She stops herself.)*.

BEE: But you don't like her. You're always complaining about her. Just because what?

EM: I do. I'm not. Alright, she can be a bit –

BEE: Just because what?

EM: Look, she'll be back in a minute. /Can't you just –

BEE: Oh god. This is a nightmare.

EM: It needn't be.

BEE: It is.

EM: Just look on it as an opportunity.

BEE: Will you stop being so fucking Zen.

EM: I am a Buddhist.

BEE: Well, don't be.

EM: Bee, why are we arguing? We don't argue.

CHRIS returns waving two bottles of wine.

CHRIS: Look what I found. Salvation. /There are bottles and bottles of the stuff out there.

EM: Nononono that's not ours.

CHRIS: What?

EM: I'm afraid it's not ours.

CHRIS: Well whose is it then?

EM: Raph's.

CHRIS: Oh Raph won't mind, bless him. He won't miss a bottle /or two, whoever he is.

She starts rummaging around in drawers for a corkscrew.

EM: No he will, he collects it, he collects wine.

CHRIS: Listen to her. Just because she's on the wagon. /
Darling, I'll replace it, don't worry.

EM: No, it's nothing to do – I promise, you can't – they're all
special. Special wines.

CHRIS: And what is this if not special? It's a reunion. It needs
celebrating.

(She produces a corkscrew. Starts to open the bottle.) Aha! You
can't hide from me, little corkscrew.

EM: Please don't Chris.

CHRIS: It's alright. You can tell him I did it. /I'll take the
blame.

EM: No, you don't understand. He collects them. They're not
for drinking yet.

CHRIS: Oh please. 'Not for drinking yet.' They're here. We're
here. It's France. And I'm thirsty. É voila.

CHRIS fills two glasses and offers one to BEE. She hesitates.

CHRIS: Oh don't you bloody start. Look, I've opened it now.
I'll only drink the stuff on my own if you don't have some.
Here. Take it.

After a moment, BEE accepts it. EM exhales meaningfully.

CHRIS: Cheers. Friends.

BEE drinks virtually the whole glass down in one go.

BEE: Frasier.

CHRIS looks blank, then gets it, laughs.

CHRIS: Course, Friday night. Cheers, Friends, Frasier… Not
that I'm in that often on a Friday night, but, you know. Em,
you look like somebody's just died. For goodness' sake,
woman. Eat, drink and re-marry, for tomorrow – it's wine,
just wine.

EM: Irreplacable. It's /irreplacable.

CHRIS: And what are friends if not irreplacable? I will buy
him another bottle of Chateau de whatever it is, roll

it around in the dust a bit and he'll never know the difference.

BEE: Why'd you change your name?

CHRIS: What?

BEE: Why'd you change your name?

CHRIS: Why did you change your accent?

BEE: I've not changed my accent.

CHRIS: You sound almost English. It's not meant to be an insult.

BEE: I've not been home in a while.

CHRIS: So you live…?

BEE: In London.

CHRIS: London? And what is it you do? Em did tell me, but I'm afraid – management consultant was it?

EM: /Logistics.

BEE: Logistics consultant.

CHRIS: That's right, yeah. Logistics. *(Pause.)* What does that mean then?

EM: It's very high powered.

CHRIS: I'm sure it is. Something to do with logic, is it?

BEE: Something, yeah.

CHRIS: Go on.

BEE: Well, we deal with corporate events mostly, the practical aspects.

CHRIS: Who goes where, that kind of thing.

BEE: Yes.

CHRIS: And?

BEE: I investigate the facilities – you want to know this?

CHRIS: Go on, yes.

BEE: Investigate the facilities required to organise an event, which will involve setting up databases, ensuring that travel arrangements dovetail with timetables and basically managing the non-infrastructural aspects of a project – that is to say, those areas which aren't germaine – central – to the project itself.

CHRIS: I'm not stupid.

Pause.

BEE: Did I say you were?

CHRIS: I know what infrastructure is. And germaine.

BEE: I was just elaborating.

EM: It's beyond me, whatever it is. I mean, she actually runs the company, you know, she's amazing.

CHRIS: Funny, I always thought you would have done something more creative, you know, you were always so good at English.

EM: So were you.

CHRIS: Mrs. Cramer, she hated me though, didn't she. Locking me in the storage cupboard, old cow. I'm sure that's illegal.

EM: And me she did, /and I wasn't even doing anything. She did!

CHRIS: No she didn't.

EM: Well not the storage one, no, the other one, you know the other one with all the brooms and cloths and cleaning stuff.

CHRIS: The cleaning cupboard.

EM: Exactly. /And all I was doing, I was laughing – shuttup – I just got

CHRIS: The one with the brooms!

EM: the giggles like I used to, because you'd set up all these drawing pins on her chair and when she sat down /nothing happened.

27

CHRIS: Nothing happened, that's right, we, yeah, we thought they must've gone up her crack, nowhere else they could have gone, and we were wetting ourselves. So she put us in the cupboard. But she never mentioned the drawing pins, did she? That was the thing. She never said anything. Probably still there. Do you remember that, Bee? Ooh, bread, cheese and wine. What more could we want?

BEE speaks with an intensity and venom which is at odds with the level of conversation.

BEE: *Of course I remember you fucking witch. I remember everything.*

CHRIS: A french waiter with little bijoux buttocks would be nice I suppose, but you can't have everything.

BEE: Did I –

Pause.

CHRIS: What?

BEE: Nothing.

Silence. Set back to:

CHRIS: We thought they must've gone up her crack, nowhere else they could have gone, and we were wetting ourselves. So she put us in the cupboard. But she never mentioned the drawing pins, did she? That was the thing. She never said anything. Probably still there. Do you remember that, Bee? Ooh, bread, cheese and wine. What more could we want? *(Pause.)* A french waiter with little bijoux buttocks would be nice I suppose, but you can't have everything.

BEE: Did I –

Pause.

CHRIS: What?

BEE: Nothing.

Silence.

CHRIS: Do you see each other quite a bit then?

BEE: Yes.

CHRIS: Lovely house, isn't it, they've got?

BEE: Gorgeous.

EM: I normally visit Bee actually. In London.

CHRIS: Oh, you normally visit her?

EM: I like the excuse. A day in town, you know.

CHRIS: Exactly, yeah, and it's a long way out, isn't it, a long drive.

EM: And that way I force her to stop working for a couple of minutes too.

CHRIS: So you haven't seen much of Cob then?

EM: She hasn't seen much of Cob, *I* haven't seen much of Cob. He's been halfway round the world and back since Christmas. Martha referred to him as 'that man with the suitcase' the other day. 'When's that man with the suitcase coming back?' That's why he's taken time off to look after them.

CHRIS: He's looking after them?

EM: Yeah. The godmother offered so we could go away together. But he's been missing them so much he said you go and I'll stay.

CHRIS: You're their godmother?

BEE: Louis'.

CHRIS: Louis' godmother?

BEE: Yes.

CHRIS: Oh right.

Pause.

CHRIS: Did I tell you, 'the jerk' and I split up?

EM: Sorry?

CHRIS: The jerk – Tim. /He kept going on and on about his ex-wife, I

EM: Oh, the jerk, yes.

CHRIS: thought oh, I've had enough of this crap, then we went on holiday, this was the final straw, and this old couple started talking to us and said 'are you married?' and he said 'yes' (because he's not actually divorced yet) and they said 'how long have you been married?'and he said 'three years today' and they looked at me and went 'aah, your wedding anniversary, how lovely'. I could have killed him.

EM laughs.

EM: Where do you get them? I never meet them, her boyfriends, this is the amazing thing. /In all these years I have never – exactly. But

CHRIS: Turnover's too quick.

EM: why were you with him anyway? That's what I don't get. You said you never even liked him.

CHRIS: Oh, the jerk was one of those people you go out with thinking it'll pass the time of day and suddenly a year's gone by and all you've done is bugger about playing 'who's the king of the castle?', you know what I mean? Anyway, I gave him a fantastic send off.

EM: What?

CHRIS: Before I left, you'll like this one, before I left, I got hold of the fattest piece of steak, biggest lump of raw beef I could find, right, and sewed it into the back of his sofa.

EM: Why?

CHRIS: Think about it.

Pause.

EM: Oh my god, no, that's disgusting. Oh my god.

BEE stands up suddenly, looking nauseous. She seems about to say something, but grabs her glass and downs it instead.

The lights go. Darkness. A beat.

EM: Oh not again.

CHRIS: What's going on?

BEE: Shit.

EM: Sorry. Sorry about this. They keep tripping.

BEE: Where's that bloody fuse box?

EM: Above the door.

BEE makes her way towards the door.

CHRIS: Tripping? What do you mean, tripping?

BEE stumbles.

BEE: Ow!

EM: Falling over.

They laugh.

BEE: Shuttup, I'm trying to, bloody bags in the way.

EM: They get overloaded, you turn on one thing too many.

BEE: Which side?

EM: Left.

BEE: There's nothing on the left.

EM: Right then.

CHRIS: Gosh, it's all a bit third world, isn't it?

BEE: There are two switches. There's one with a –

The lights come back on. BEE re-enters.

EM: Yes, that one. Well done. He hasn't sorted out the electrics properly yet.

CHRIS: How primitive. Reminds me of the miners' strikes. All those blackouts and candles.

CHRIS starts to open another bottle.

EM: No, Chris, don't open another one!

CHRIS: As easy to replace two as one. Why aren't you drinking anyway? Is it un-Buddhist to drink? No, I'm not being funny, I don't know, it might be. Muslims don't.

EM: I've given up because Bee wanted to give up smoking.

CHRIS: That's nice.

EM: I thought it would help if we did it together.

BEE: I'm sorry. You gave up because you wanted to give up.

CHRIS: You don't drink that much, do you?

EM: No, I wanted to feel less tired, that's all, I mean, no, not that much, but I just thought it would be a good time to try.

BEE: *(Under her breath.)* 'Thought it would help'. Jesus.

EM: Bridg.

BEE: What?

EM: How much more are you going to drink?

BEE: Don't fucking patronise me! I'm thirty two. I will not be patronised!

Silence. BEE helps herself to another glass which she gulps down.

CHRIS: You swear.

BEE: What?

CHRIS: You never used to swear.

BEE: You talking about?

CHRIS: You used to say 'goolies'. Do you remember? She used to go, something terrible would happen, she'd go 'oh goolies, my nail's broken!' Or – what was it? 'Plonker!' – that was the other one. If you were really pissed off with someone – 'you plonker!' That was the worst it got. 'Plonker and goolies.' So sweet.

BEE: Is that right?

CHRIS: Except not that sweet actually because what you were actually saying is cock and bollocks. If I've got my biology right.

BEE: I can't say I remember.

CHRIS: And biology was, after all, biology was, I don't know how, the only O'Level I did better than you in, wasn't it? No thanks to that old bastard, Mr. Kanani. You remember that lesson where we all had to jump up and down, then try and find our pulses, on the wrist, he said, on the wrist, and I couldn't find mine, so he got me outside and stuck his hand up my shirt and was going 'can you feel it now?

Can you feel it now?' God, when I think about it,
dirty old sod.

Silence.

BEE: It didn't happen to you.

CHRIS: What?

BEE: It didn't happen to you.

CHRIS: What do you mean?

BEE: It happened to me.

CHRIS: What?

BEE: Mr. Kanani. He did that to me.

CHRIS: Hang on a minute. What are you saying?

BEE: I'm saying it didn't happen to you. It happened to me.

CHRIS: I'm sorry but I – how dare you – I remember him
sticking his hand up my shirt /and trying to find my heart.

BEE: You remember me telling you and you think it happened
to you. But it didn't. It happened to me.

CHRIS looks at EM in exaggerated disbelief.

EM: Don't look at me, I can't remember.

CHRIS: I don't believe this.

Pause.

EM: It certainly didn't happen to me.

BEE: You – *(Pause.) You've re-invented yourself, haven't you?*

CHRIS: What?

BEE: *You've trained your memory so well that you've actually
forgotten it's cheating. Your memory is your dog and you can make
it stay, fetch or shit on other people's flower beds as you please.
Oh, to have a memory that only comes when it's called.*

EM: Maybe it happened to both of you.

*BEE stares at EM, then walks out, picking up CHRIS's cigarettes,
unseen, as she goes. She closes the glass door behind her.*

CHRIS: Oh dear.

BEE returns. Set back to:

BEE: You remember me telling you and you think it happened to you. But it didn't. It happened to me.

CHRIS looks at EM in exaggerated disbelief.

EM: Don't look at me, I can't remember.

CHRIS: I don't believe this.

Pause.

EM: It certainly didn't happen to me.

BEE: You –

Silence.

CHRIS: What?

EM: Maybe it happened to both of you.

BEE stares at EM, then walks out, picking up CHRIS's cigarettes, unseen, as she goes. She closes the glass door behind her.

CHRIS: Oh dear.

EM: She's a bit fragile at the moment.

CHRIS: As if I'd make it up. Honestly. *(Pause.)* Why?

EM: Tired. Overworked.

CHRIS: She does look dreadful. Not pregnant is she?

EM: No. Why?

CHRIS: That sort of emotional state. You know.

EM: No, she's not.

CHRIS: She might be, /you never know.

EM: She's not pregnant.

Silence.

EM: What I like about this place, you can smell things growing.

CHRIS: God she's changed though.

EM: Some days, at home, I swear I'm so busy I forget to breathe.

CHRIS: Don't you think she has? It's like a /different person completely. I mean has she shrunk? I remember her as taller somehow.

EM: Hmm?

CHRIS: Still as nervous as a fucking racehorse though. She doesn't know, does she?

EM: What?

CHRIS: About me coming here. That we planned –

EM: Course not, no! Anyway, I wasn't expecting you to just, you know –

CHRIS: She got a man?

EM: No.

CHRIS: And no kids?

EM: No.

Pause.

EM: God, I love it here. It seems so far away from all the trivia. This countryside, it's something else.

CHRIS: There's an awful lot of countryside in France, isn't there?

EM: Mm.

CHRIS: But I look at it, I'm afraid, I do, and I think, yes, but what's it for?

EM: For?

CHRIS: All that space. What's the point of it? It's the lack of people which unnerves me.

EM: In France?

CHRIS: No, in the countryside. It's so…barren. Give me cities, people, life, any day. You know what the countryside reminds me of? Death.

EM: Nature is a reflection, just a reflection of your inner self.

CHRIS: So I'm dead.

EM: So you're projecting your own morbidity onto it.

CHRIS: You know, the funny thing, you were never that religious at school, were you? It was her, you just went along with it because of her, didn't you? And now you're a raving Buddhist and – is she still religious then, as well?

EM: I am not raving. /No, she's not. /And anyway, what has this got to

CHRIS: Well you know what I mean.

EM: do with religion, I'm just talking about nature.

CHRIS: Well I was just wondering, it just made me think about her being your godmother, I mean Louis' godmother, if that was why, because you've never mentioned it before and, well I didn't even realise you saw that much of her, to be honest.

EM: She's my oldest friend.

CHRIS: Right. Right, yeah, of course. *(Silence.)* She never asked me what I did. Did you notice that? I don't mind. It's not as if I want to talk about my high powered job in fucking telephone sales, you know, but you'd think, wouldn't you, after all these years, you'd think she might ask.

EM: She's a bit preoccupied at the moment.

Pause.

CHRIS: You're sure she's not pregnant?

EM: You keep saying that. No, she can't be. *(She spots BEE smoking on the verandah.)* Oh, for goodness' sake!

CHRIS: What? What?

EM: Now she's smoking.

CHRIS: Oh god /I thought something terrible – *(She notices her cigarettes are gone.)* Hey!

EM: What is going on?

CHRIS: They're mine. She's nicked my fags!

EM: Stay here/ and I'll – you just stay here.

CHRIS: Cheeky cow. At least tell her to save me one, will you, darling.

EM goes out to BEE.

CHRIS snoops around, eventually comes across the music system and goes through the tape collection.

EM: Bee, you're smoking.

BEE: I was at a conference last week. Big building, thirty eight floors.

EM: Stop it, stop it! Take it out!

BEE: I had to walk up and down the stairs six times one day.

EM: STOP SMOKING!

BEE: 'Why don't you take the lift?' 'Is it for the exercise?' they said.

EM: It doesn't calm you down. See. It does nothing to calm you down.

BEE: 'Because I'm claustrophobic', I said. Why am I claustrophobic?

EM: For God's sake Bee, /you haven't even given up for twelve hours.

BEE: Why am I claustrophobic, Em?

EM: You've drunk half Raph's wine cellar. What is wrong with you?

BEE: Why am I claustrophobic?

EM: You asking me? *(Pause.)* I don't know.

BEE *(Softly.)* Jesus Christ.

EM: What?

BEE: You sit there, reminiscing like we're old friends –

EM: We are old friends. /That's what we are.

BEE: Oh and what definition of friend would you be using there?

EM: Bee –

BEE: Friend, as in evil fucking cow.

EM: I really think – look, I know sometimes she can be a bit
– but we were friends, Bee, we did everything together.

BEE: A bit what? A bit what? You know, Emma, when you
have children – you told me this – when you have children
you lose, what is it? Thirty percent of your brain. That's
what's happened. You've forgotten – the part that held
all the childhood memories – it's gone. Wshhhsh. The
database has been erased.

EM: Don't fucking tell me what I have or haven't forgotten.
Don't you dare! Your memory is as selective as the rest of
ours, yes it is, we all do – you want a fight, have it with her,
not me. Do not pick your fight with me. But I thought – I
would have thought you might, after all these years, just be
ready to let it go. And don't point that bloody cigarette at
me. *(Silence.)* Anyway, it comes back.

BEE: What?

EM: Thirty percent of your brain. It comes back.

Pause.

BEE: When?

EM: Oh fuck off.

BEE: No you fuck off

EM: No you fuck off, Bee Hannon, because it doesn't matter
what I remember. Ask her.

BEE: Of course it matters what you remember. You were there.

EM: Ask her. Talk to her. She's the one you can't forgive.

BEE: Oh is that what this is about? Is that why she's here? So I
can forgive her and we can all play skipping games again?

EM: She just turned up! I didn't bloody know she was coming,
did I?

BEE: Didn't you?

EM: No!

Suddenly: the opening bars of 'River deep, mountain high' fill the stage.

CHRIS has found the tape she wanted.

BEE: Oh god, no.

CHRIS starts to dance. She opens the glass doors and dances towards EM and BEE. BEE sinks into her chair.

CHRIS is a bit of a disco queeen. EM laughs, enjoying her performance.

She entertains EM with a virtuoso sequence, then EM suddenly jumps up to join her. They revive an old routine together, then go their own ways, dancing around the room.

CHRIS crosses to BEE and tries to force her up to dance. BEE refuses. There's a bit of a struggle, then CHRIS abandons BEE to finish the song with EM. They collapse, exhausted and laughing, in a heap.

BEE strides over to turn off the music.

CHRIS: Oh no don't Bee! What is it? Oh god, I'm sorry, darling, I forgot you can't dance. That's why – she can't dance, can she? Oh shame.

Silence. BEE looks like she might cry. But she draws herself up instead.

BEE: It was a game at first. Burying things. Your gerbil. Then the bird we found behind my sofa. And the ceremonies got more and more elaborate. We sang hymns, said prayers, and you'd give the lesson, which was basically always the same; 'be kind to little animals, or they will bite you.' Then we buried the bee. In a matchbox. And I said 'I'm Bee, so I should bury the bee', and you gave me a strange look and said, 'go on then' and I did and then you started digging the hole. At first I thought we were making a den. But you wouldn't say and we had to dig for days, you wouldn't play anything else. 'It's not big enough yet', you kept saying. *(Pause.)* Am I talking out loud?

CHRIS: What?

BEE: Am I –

EM: Yes.

Pause.

BEE: We were laughing when you lowered me into the hole, it was still a game. And then you covered me in earth. And I could hear you singing a hymn over me. Then it was silent. All quiet for so long I thought I must be dead. When you took me out – when you took me out – when you took me out you said I was disgusting. The smell of mud was not enough to disguise the smell of shit. And you dropped me back in the hole. So I must've climbed out on my own. *(Silence.)* How was I supposed to breathe?

CHRIS: Well that's a jolly little story, isn't it? Bloody hell, just because you can't dance.

BEE: How was I supposed to breathe?

CHRIS: What?

BEE: *How was I supposed to breathe?*

CHRIS: Jesus, I don't know! This is years ago.

BEE: You dug a hole and buried me and you don't know why.

CHRIS: I didn't say that.

BEE: Why?

CHRIS: I can't remember why we put you in a bloody hole. What is this?!

BEE: Not 'we'. You. You dug the hole. It was your idea.

CHRIS: We were kids for god's sake! I don't know!

BEE: I'm not interested in who pulled whose hair in Geography, or what Mr. Kanani did in Biology, I'm interested in whether you remember, whether you remember what you did to me.

Pause.

EM: The thing is, we all remember different things, don't we? I mean, different things stand out for each of us, and I think what Bee is trying to say, I mean we shared our past, but that's not to say it was the same past. I mean, you share an apple, you get different bits of the same apple, don't you? Pips, no pips, core, stick, whatever, but it's the same apple. And in her memory, in Bee's memory, there are things which happened and I think what she wants is to find out whether, in your memory, they happened. As well. Is that right? Bee, would you say that's right?

BEE: I know what I remember. I want to know what she remembers. That's all.

CHRIS: What I remember? You want to know what I remember?

Silence, so long, that you might think CHRIS has forgotten the question.

CHRIS: One morning as the sun lit
Up a beach in Donegal
I wandered from the house there
With my bucket, spade and ball.

I found a little cove
Between the cliffside and the sea
And shouted out into the wind
'It's me it's me it's me'.

A funny looking crab
Sidled up along the sand
It circled round me twice
Before it settled on my hand.

I made a castle for him
And put him in the moat
Then turned the bucket upside down
And used it as a boat.

He didn't really like that
And so I let him go
But as I did a seagull
Came and nibbled at my toe.

The great big puffy bird looked
Right up at me and said

'Good morning, little girl,
What are you doing out of bed?'

I ran home by the rock pool,
And tiptoed past the cave.
Looked back upon the sea
Who gave me one last wave.

But sitting in the kitchen
All my mother said to me
Was 'you haven't washed your face, girl'
And 'do you need a wee?'

*EM laughs. BEE looks uncertain. She refills her empty glass. CHRIS
holds hers out for refilling. BEE fills it.*

EM: It's lovely. Did you write it?

CHRIS: Remember that, Bee?

EM: Did Bee write it?

CHRIS: She did.

EM: It's lovely, a lovely poem.

BEE: I did?

CHRIS: You did.

EM: It's so good. *(To CHRIS.)* And for you to remember it, my
    god!

CHRIS: Do you remember?

BEE: No.

EM: To retain all that. How? The only thing I can retain is
    water.

BEE *(To CHRIS.)* Why?

EM: Once a month, you know. Period. But how do you
    memorise it all? I could never – I can't even remember
    nursery rhymes. They're always telling me off – I'll start
    one, you know, like 'ding dong dell, pussy's in the well,
    who put her in? Little Johnny Green' and then I can't
    remember who took him out, can I? 'Who took him out?

Ladidadida.' I trail off, hoping they're not listening but they always are.

BEE: Why?

CHRIS: Because it was good. *(Pause.)* You were always good at English. Words. Syllogisms. We used to love messing about with those, didn't we?

EM: Syllogisms.

CHRIS: Yes, logic, you know, she used to doodle them all over the place. My cat likes fish. Fish smell. My cat smells. That kind of thing.

EM: Cats don't smell though, do they, they're very clean.

CHRIS: And we used to have this game, you were brilliant at it, you remember, where you'd have three words and you'd make a story out of them, you know, like, I don't know, like leaf, golf ball and sofa. And you'd just make up these amazing stories. Can you still do that? Leaf, golf ball and sofa, go on.

BEE: No.

CHRIS: Or something else, say, holiday, satchel and foetus. How about that? Foetus, holiday and satchel.

Silence. EM breaks it suddenly, deliberately.

EM: And do you remember that language we made up? EMTE. Where you'd go 'Fritancite'. France. 'Fritancite itin thite itautitumn' Ha! Itautitumn! I like that.

CHRIS: Yes, but –

EM: Hiterite wite itarite titogitethiter itagitain. I can still do it! Remember, /you go 'it' before every vowel.

CHRIS: Yes, but Bee didn't know it, did she? She wasn't there.

EM: Oh didn't we all –? I could have sworn –

CHRIS: No. It was when she was off school that time.

EM: And why did we call it that then? EMTE?

CHRIS: Your initials, my initials.

EM: Oh yes. Oh yes, of course. But you know, this is what
amazes me, they all do it. You think it's original, don't you,
at that age, you think you're the only ones, that you're so
clever, but Louis – eleven years old he is and he's started,
he's already started with this made-up language, he does
it with this particular friend, they start gibbering and he
loves the fact that I don't know what they're on about,
he just loves it, the little bugger. They come in, him and
his friend, and this boy, Ed, keeps going 'I nac ees roy
srekin' every time I see him, it's so annoying, I mean I
could easily, if I wanted, I could easily work out what
they're saying, but I can't be bothered, wittering away
about trainers or gameboy or whatever it is, because they
have this life, you see, this other life suddenly, and you're
expected to – I don't know what. Skivvy. Shuttup and do
the dishes. And then you're wheeled in for a bit of maths
homework (which, in my case is a joke, of course) but
you're *no fun* any more. What you are, what you become to
them, it has nothing to do with fun. I'm not complaining.
Because of course in Tom's case I'm still a walking breast
and Martha's only just out of nappies so there's all that, but
sometimes – I mean, even Martha, I said to her the other
week, she wouldn't wear this lovely yellow dress because
her friend Morgan apparently doesn't like yellow and I
said 'it doesn't matter what other people think. It's what
you think that matters'. A few days later she wouldn't put
on this hat and we had this argument; 'Why not?' 'Don't
like it.' 'Well I love it' I said. 'I don't care what you think.
It's what I think that matters'. I felt about as big as the gap
under the door. I mean, God, I love them to death, but
sometimes it just feels like need, rejection, need, rejection,
nothing inbetween you know, nothing adult – well, Cob
obviously – but when you're shovelling cold baked beans
in your mouth straight from the tin because you just
haven't got time, and your clothes are covered in crap and
back to front, you think, hang on, hang on a minute, what
about me? What about me? I'm not complaining, it's just,
it's just.... *(She stops suddenly in mid-thought.)* back to front, of

course, it's back to front! 'I nac ees roy srekin'. 'I can...see...
your...knickers', oh god, 'I can see your knickers' back to
front, 'I nac ees roy srekin.'

*EM begins to laugh. The laugh gets louder and longer until it's out
of control. And then, to the amazement of BEE and CHRIS, it turns
into a wail, and EM cries uncontrollably.*

BEE goes to comfort her.

BEE: Hey hey hey hey.

EM: Oh god, I'm sorry, /I just – how ridiculous –

BEE: It's okay, it's alright.

EM: No I really – oh I can't stop now.

BEE: Don't worry, Em, you just relax, /it's fine.

CHRIS: Would you like – should I get some – thing?

EM: How embarrassing. /I completely – how embarrassing.

BEE: It's not embarrassing. We're friends. Here, come here.

EM: What did I do? Oh, look at me, I can't stop crying.

BEE embraces her until her crying subsides.

EM: Oh, dear me.

CHRIS: You alright now?

EM: I don't know where that came from.

BEE: It's okay. /We all need to lose it sometimes.

EM: I think I'd better – euch, make-up all over my face. /I'll
just go –

BEE: Just relax. It doesn't matter.

EM: no, I'll just go and sort myself out. God, I must be more
tired than I thought. No, I will, I must. How ridiculous.

She goes. Silence.

CHRIS: I've never seen her do that before. Have you seen her
do that before?

BEE: No.

CHRIS: No, nor have I.

BEE: I've never seen anyone do that before.

CHRIS: She went, *(She laughs.)* she started laughing –

BEE: It was like a wave.

CHRIS: Yeah, she started and she couldn't stop, /she lost control of the laugh –

BEE: It was like, it was like a god-almighty wave, where you know – even as it starts on up – you know it's going to come crashing down again in a minute.

CHRIS: And drown her.

BEE: And drown her. You couldn't say where the laugh stopped and the crying started. 'Twas a flurry of foam and spray.

CHRIS: It was the undertow.

BEE: That's right, she got caught by the undertow.

CHRIS: I had no idea she was so upset.

BEE: It came from nowhere. The undertow.

CHRIS: It's probably the marital thing.

BEE: What marital thing?

CHRIS: And why isn't she drinking? Is that why she isn't drinking? She's hardly an alcoholic, is she? She's probably just down – if I don't drink for a few days I go right down, plummet.

BEE: What marital thing?

CHRIS: Or maybe it's post-natal. Could be. Bit late. But it could be.

BEE: What marital thing?

CHRIS: Oh, you know, they were having a few problems, arguments, with him being away so much. That's when he said the thing about needing space.

BEE: 'Needing space'?

CHRIS: Yes, the problem is it seems they all have to adjust every time he comes back, but they can't relax because they know he's off again. So she said she wanted to spend time together, just the two of them, and he came out with this thing about needing his own space.

BEE: When?

CHRIS: Oh this was a few months ago now.

BEE: Space?

CHRIS: Well, exactly. 'Space'. What does that mean? Means he's fucking someone else, in my book. *(Silence.)* Sorry, I thought she would have told you.

BEE: You mean he is?

CHRIS: Yes.

BEE: She told you this? *(CHRIS nods.)* He's having an affair?

CHRIS: I'm sure he is. Or was. All the signs.

BEE: But hang on, hang on, did she say – she didn't *say* he was? /She didn't actually say he was?

CHRIS: She didn't say he was, no, not in so many words, but –

BEE: No, so she didn't actually say anything to you?

CHRIS: No, but I'm not stupid.

BEE: Jesus Christ.

CHRIS: What?

BEE: Yes you are. You're a fucking idiot. You just…make things up, don't you? Just make them up.

CHRIS: *I am not stupid. (Silence.)* Have you seen Cob lately then?

(BEE doesn't answer.) When did you last see him?

BEE: Why?

CHRIS: No, I just wondered.

BEE: Why?

CHRIS: Only being so close to Em it must be difficult. I mean obviously it's all understood and in the past and all that, but even so. I've often wondered. She's never said anything about it to me, but what did she say when you told her? About you and Cob?

BEE: Jesus Christ, she's next door.

CHRIS: So?

BEE: Are you *mad*?

CHRIS: You mean she doesn't know?

BEE: Of course she doesn't know.

CHRIS: Well that's not very fucking honest of you, is it?!

Silence.

BEE: What do you want from me?

CHRIS: It did occur to me that she didn't know, the fact that you're still so close. But then I thought, no, how could they be these best friends they're supposed to be with that kind of a secret between them? I don't want anything from you. I didn't come to see you, did I? I came to see my friend.

BEE: She's not your friend.

CHRIS: What?

BEE: She's not your friend.

CHRIS: Oh very mature.

BEE: You want to know what she thinks of you?

CHRIS: No.

BEE: She pities you. She puts up with you because she's kind. She feels sorry for you, like she would for a chicken the fox half ate and left for dead. You turn up when you've lost a job or a boyfriend, you call her when you're depressed. And she's nice to you because that's what she is. Nice. She's a nice person. Kind. She's a fucking angel. But you don't *know* her, do you? You don't know what makes her cry, or laugh, you don't know, you never even remember, that she's a vegetarian, all these years, and you still ask, every time you see her, whether she'd prefer chicken or lamb, and this is a woman who'd rather eat her own legs than a chicken's, because you think you're so bloody interesting with your endless hangovers and diets and your tight trousers and your fucking strangers in toilets and your stupid B movie life. You just moan or boast, boast or moan. And she just listens. That's not friendship, it's counselling and she has had enough.

CHRIS: Is that so?

BEE: It is so.

Silence.

BEE: And if you ever told her, it would destroy her.

CHRIS: What? *(Pause.)* No, it would destroy your relationship with her. She'd be fine.

BEE: It would destroy her.

Silence.

CHRIS: We were friends once. You and me. Funny, isn't it, the way things change.

BEE: Nothing has changed. We were never friends.

CHRIS: We were friends, fuck it, you can't just go round saying we weren't when we quite obviously were.

BEE: We did things together. /That's all.

CHRIS: We did everything together. We lived in each others' bloody pop socks.

BEE: And what, for the love of god, was friendly about rubbing my face in the mud? About sitting on me and rubbing my face in the dirt because I was wearing the wrong shoes or skirt or I had the same fucking watch as you? /And what was friendly about clubbing

CHRIS: Oh come on.

BEE: anyone who tried to talk to me when you decided, for no reason, that I was not to be spoken to? About sending me to Coventry for three and a half weeks? And then having me beg, to get down on my knees and beg in front of everyone to be allowed to speak, so that I might be your friend again? You were a fucking cunt, and here you are, you walk in the door like you belong here. You make me want to throw up. What in god's name is friendly about that?

CHRIS: All these things /you say –

BEE: And where did you get that poem anyway? They were mine, my poems were mine.

CHRIS: You didn't even recognise it.

BEE: Where did you get it?

CHRIS: Copied it. From that book of yours.

BEE: You took my book?

CHRIS: What?

BEE: You took my book?

CHRIS: No. Copied it, I said. I copied it. And other ones. They were good. 'Yellow Socks'. 'Half Moon Arising'. 'The Day Before Yesterday'. And some of the short stories I remember too. Not as good, but still, for that age.

BEE: *(Softly.)* Christ.

CHRIS: What?

BEE: Why?

CHRIS: I told you. *(Pause.)* They were good.

BEE: Good?

CHRIS: They were.

BEE: Good.

CHRIS: Yes, good for fuck's sake!

BEE: You copied them because they were good.

CHRIS: Yes yes yes!

BEE: You stole my book /and copied them – alright, borrowed my book

CHRIS: I gave it back, no, I gave it back.

BEE: and copied them because they were good.

CHRIS: Fucking YES!

BEE: I don't get it.

CHRIS: Oh for crying out loud, what do you think? Because I wanted to steal your soul? Because I wanted to sell them, make my million?!

(They stare at each other. Finally it's CHRIS who turns away.)

Christ!

There's a crash from upstairs. BEE looks up, but CHRIS is too absorbed in her thoughts to notice. BEE calls up the stairs.

BEE: Em? Em! *(No answer. She mutters to herself.)* What is she up to?

She leaves and goes on up the stairs.

CHRIS is unaware of her having left. After a moment, she continues talking.

CHRIS: Because you were better than me. That's all. You were always better than me. Happy now? *(Silence. CHRIS looks round. There's nobody there.)*

Well FUCK YOU BEE HANNON!

CHRIS grabs the wine bottle, pours herself another glass, then throws the bottle over the verandah. She gulps down the wine.

BEE and EM re-enter.

EM: I fell asleep. Just sat down, fell asleep, like an old woman, sitting up in the chair. And then I must have have lolled over to one side, hit the sidetable and crashed onto the floor, god, I didn't know *where* I was, thought I was the only survivor in an aircrash for a minute, I must have been dreaming. Had no idea I was that tired.

Silence. CHRIS makes no response.

BEE Shall we call you a taxi?

CHRIS: No, I'm fine, thank you.

BEE: Jesus Christ, if you're not going, I am.

CHRIS: Haven't you got something to tell Em first?

Silence.

EM: What? *(Pause.)* What? Oh, stop it. Nervous tension. /You're going to set me off again.

CHRIS: We've been talking about friendship, Em, you know, how well you can know someone and yet some things – it's funny, isn't it? – how there can still be some things you don't know about them. On the other hand, I haven't seen Bee in years and yet in many ways it's like yesterday.

EM: What are you talking about?

Pause.

CHRIS: If you don't tell her, I will.

Silence. CHRIS addresses BEE.

CHRIS: Alright, okay, I'll help you. It's not that I haven't thought about you in eighteen years. You pop up, now and again, you've popped up. Couple of years ago I had a termination reminded me of you. This guy I met, complete tosser, even while we were doing it I thought 'this isn't going to happen again, darling, not if you don't get a bloody move on', you know, like trying to get it on with a tube of playdoh. So I was just getting to the point of saying 'I think I'd be better off on my own, thank you' and before I know it he's in there, no condom, nothing, and I'm up the spout. What amazed me though, my god, is what happened to these though. *(She indicates her breasts.)* Suddenly I'm knocking things off tabletops every time I turn round. Only bit about it I liked. Smart outfit though, this clinic. Not like the one I found you. Mr. Hirangi with his grey pumps and his dandruff, god, I remember thinking that, how can you be a doctor and have dandruff? Anyway, I'm sorry to hear you can't have children. Was it because of the abortion? Infection in the tubes or something, because I know that can happen. *(Silence. BEE stares at CHRIS, then at EM.)* No, she didn't tell me. I guessed.

BEE: Get out of here. *(CHRIS remains where she is.)* GET OUT OF HERE! GET OUT OF MY…

CHRIS: It's not your house, darling.

BEE: Life.

Pause.

CHRIS: Tell her.

Silence. BEE addresses EM.

BEE: Do you remember the time I broke my wrist? At school? On the way home from school?

CHRIS: What's this got to do with anything?

BEE: Em?

EM: Yes.

BEE: You were there, weren't you?

EM: Yes.

BEE: I've never lied to you, Em.

EM: I don't understand.

BEE addresses CHRIS.

BEE: I'm walking in front of you and you're calling me a fat ugly duck and you keep poking my shoulder with a stick.

CHRIS: What's this got /to do with anything?

BEE: You say I don't know how to walk properly, my posture's useless, so I'm carrying your bag as well as mine, one on each shoulder, to 'even me out', you say, /and then you start this chant: 'shoulders

CHRIS: This isn't what we were talking about. I don't know what –

BEE: back, head up, beak out', *shuttup!* 'shoulders back, head up, beak out' and then I stop because the bags are slipping off and you walk smack into me, knock me over. I land on my wrist which makes a cracking sound and it's cold on the pavement and it stinks, but I don't move. I won't move. I want to stay there. You're screaming at me to get up. You don't touch me, help me, just scream and scream and then all of a sudden you stop. Then I hear someone laughing. Laughing uncontrollably, and I realise it's me. The lollipop man helps me up. You've gone. But I catch sight of you in the distance. You're walking so fast your heels don't touch down, and you're cradling your bag like a baby. Your shoulders are *even*. Then you cross the road and you see me. I know you've seen me because you look 'left, right' and you don't look left again – just step out into the road. Right into the path of a yellow lorry which runs you quietly over. It stops. Then reverses. Forward, then back. Forward, then back. Three times until I can't distinguish you from the road. And I'm weeping for joy on the grass verge. *(Silence.)* Only this last bit is fantasy, obviously, because you're here, now.

CHRIS: What are you talking about?

BEE: I'm talking about what I would like to have happened.

CHRIS: This has nothing to do with anything, Em, I don't know what she's going on about.

BEE: There are some things you can't forget and some you don't want to remember. I am not a liar. *(She addresses CHRIS.)* But you are a *witch*.

CHRIS: Tell her. Go on, tell her for god's sake.

EM: What is it?

CHRIS: Tell her about you and Cob.

BEE: *(Softly.)* Christ.

Silence. EM sits down, takes her time.

EM: God you must think I'm stupid.

Silence.

CHRIS: Why?

EM: I mean, I know I'm stupid. Academically. But that doesn't mean I'm unaware. I've always been aware.

CHRIS: You knew?

EM nods. Silence.

BEE: Hang on a minute, hang on. Let's all just sit down and – here.

BEE puts a hand out for a cigarette.

CHRIS: You bloody sit down. What?

BEE: Cigarette.

CHRIS: Fuck off.

BEE rolls her eyes, looks back to EM.

EM: Why do you think we asked you to be godmother?

BEE: Because I'm your best friend. *(Pause.)* /And you knew –

EM: And I knew why you couldn't have children.

Silence.

EM: Yes.

BEE: You never said. Anything.

EM: It was a long time ago.

BEE: How long have you known?

EM: Since I was pregnant. With Louis.

BEE: Eleven years.

EM: Twelve, yes.

BEE: Twelve. *(Pause.)* He told you?

EM: I guessed.

BEE: You guessed?

EM: Mm.

BEE: What did you guess?

EM: That something had happened.

BEE: That something had happened?

EM: Yes.

BEE: What?

EM: Well, you know.

BEE: You guessed?

EM: Well he's normally so macho about that sort of thing, Cob. Illness, weakness, pregnancy. But he went all soft when I got pregnant, like he had oestrogen rushing around his body, like *he* was pregnant. And then – it was when he said he wanted me to give up work and I wasn't even past the first trimester, and he started talking about 'confinement' and I said 'what's wrong with you? You're behaving like a bloody Victorian!' And then, eventually, he told me.

Silence.

BEE: What did he tell you?

EM: To be honest, Bee, I'd rather not – you see, there was a time I thought maybe we should talk about this. When I first found out and I thought, I wished you'd bring it up and we could air it, get it out the way, but I'm not sure what the point of it is now, raking it all up again. It's so long ago.

BEE: But what did he tell you?

EM: Look, I know you don't – but there's this Zen story, and it's about – no listen – it's about living in the present, you see, in the moment, that's what I try, I'm always trying to – not to look back. So these two monks, they're on their way back from the temple when they come across this beautiful girl stranded by the roadside. It's been raining, the road's flooded, and she can't get across. The first monk, he picks her up, wades across, plonks her down, and off they go. Later that night the second monk can't control himself any longer so he says 'How could you do that? We're not supposed to look at women, let alone touch them. Especially if they're young and beautiful'. And the first monk says 'I left the girl there. Are you still carrying her?' *(Silence.)* Do you see? 'Are you still carrying her? I left the girl there?'

CHRIS: Ah, but the question is, would he have picked her up if she'd been old and ugly, eh? That's the question.

EM: No that's not the question.

BEE: I'm not sure what –

EM: Bee, it was so long ago. It doesn't matter.

BEE: It does.

EM: No, it doesn't.

BEE: It does to me.

EM: No. I forgave you both years ago. *(She embraces BEE. BEE remains impassive.)* I don't judge you, you must know that. And whatever you did, I can't imagine what it's like to know you can never have children. I can't imagine what that must be like.

BEE extricates herself from the embrace.

BEE: Forgive…me?

EM: Well of course. My god, Bee, sometimes I wonder whether you know me at all. Of course I do. I know you didn't do it to me. To hurt me. And that, for whatever reason you did it, you've suffered enough.

BEE: Em.

EM: What?

BEE: What did he tell you?

EM: Everything. He told me what happened. Just that.

BEE: But what? What did he tell you?

EM: Oh god. Alright. Alright, if you really want to – he told me that he didn't want to wait, that he couldn't wait for me, for us to get married. That's all. And that you did it once and got pregnant. That's all.

BEE: Oh god.

EM: But the thing is, Bee, no it's not all bad, because if I'd known, if I'd known at the time, I probably would have walked away, and lost you both, you see? So, sometimes, time is everything. This way I still have both my best friends, so it's alright.

BEE: No, it wasn't – we didn't – it wasn't …that.

EM: What?

Silence.

BEE: He raped me.

Silence. EM laughs.

EM: That's not funny.

BEE: I'm sorry, I'm so sorry.

CHRIS: How could you say that?

BEE: I'm so sorry, Em.

CHRIS: How could you say that? Of course he didn't *rape* her! What are you talking about?

BEE ignores CHRIS. BEE and EM look at each other.

EM suddenly turns away. She goes over to the clock, mutters to herself and turns it back. Thinks. Then puts it forward again.

She returns to the table, picks up some food, puts it to her mouth, returns it to the plate. She cannot look at BEE.

BEE: Em. Shall I go?

BEE gets up.

BEE: I'll go.

BEE's eyes rest on CHRIS. She walks up to her, slaps her hard in the face, before walking off.

CHRIS: Fucking – what's the matter with her! What did I do? What did I do? Jesus Christ! And then she takes it out on me! What does it look like? I'm going to have welts all over my bloody face now.

CHRIS finds a mirror and examines herself in it. EM paces the room, then sinks into a chair.

EM: Rape.

CHRIS: Of course he didn't rape her. Cob! He was sixteen, for god's sake, didn't know the meaning of the word. She's mad. Look at my face!

EM: Why would she lie?

CHRIS: No, she and Cob had a thing going and she never told you about it. I'm sorry, but I just think that's dishonest, even if it was years ago. A thing like that, it has to come out some time.

EM: Why would she lie to me?

CHRIS: Guilt. Must be. Guilt. So she blames him. And no one can prove it, of course, that's the thing. But I was there. I mean, not actually there, obviously, but afterwards, when she found out she was pregnant, she didn't say anything then, did she? The word wasn't mentioned then. I mean, I helped her find a clinic and all that, kept it a secret from everyone, but the word 'rape' didn't come into it.

EM: Why would she lie?

CHRIS: I have to tell you – I was quite shocked because I'm sure she never used to be – but she's a very vindictive person. She said some terrible things – this is when you were asleep – she said some terrible things about you and I thought, well, my god, you know, and they're meant to be best friends, and then I found out she'd never told you. That you'd never discussed it. Her and Cob. I was amazed. But then I thought well that's probably why. There's this thing between them, this secret. Still, it's no excuse. I mean, oh, I don't know if I should tell you this. *(Pause.)* Well it was about your attitude really. To her. She said she's always trusted you, always thought you were on her side, kind of, but she realises – and the thing about smoking is just another example really – because she realises you've just been patronising her all these years, haven't you? And that, actually, you think you're superior, don't you, she said, you think you're somehow superior. But it doesn't bother her because she thinks you're sad. With your Aga and your family values and your smug self-satisfied religion and your bloody garden with its purple sprouting broccoli and she doesn't even like Louis, she said, because he looks like Cob and reminds her of what happened, she said, I was quite shocked. *(Pause.)* Do you think my trousers are too tight?

Silence.

EM: My husband.

CHRIS: Oh fuck that. She's just a cow. Always was. And she still can't dance to save her life. Some people never change, do they? Here, let's have a bit of music then, come on, dance the cobwebs away.

CHRIS plucks a tape from the collection and puts it on. It begins in the middle of a thumping Tom Waits track.

CHRIS: Now that is what I call sexy. Yow!

She starts dancing. Then stops the tape and re-winds it. She picks up the remote control and walks over to the verandah.

CHRIS: There's only one thing to do to this music. But here we are, middle of the bloody country, three women, no men. A total non-starter that is. Although I did notice some guy on the way in though, and I thought oh he'll do, I thought, bloke on a tractor looking very gallic and phallic, he was. Do you know who I mean? Farmer or something, he must have been.

She points the remote at the music centre. There's a burst of music. She turns it off again and the tape continues to re-wind.

EM advances towards her until she is standing directly in front of her.

CHRIS: What? *(Pause.)* What?

EM contemplates CHRIS for some time. It's not clear why. Maybe they're going to embrace. Then EM takes the remote control away from CHRIS.

CHRIS: What did I say?

Swiftly and deliberately, EM pushes CHRIS backwards over the edge of the verandah. CHRIS cries out. The lights go out. Silence. The lights come back on.

EM looks over the edge of the verandah after her, curious.

BEE enters with a suitcase.

BEE: Bloody lights. *(She looks about.)* She gone? *(EM nods.)* Thank god. *(Silence. EM continues to stare over the edge.)* Em. *(EM doesn't react.)* Em. I never meant to tell you. I meant never to tell you. *(Silence.)* What are you going to do?

EM: What am I supposed to do?

BEE: Nothing.

EM: Nothing.

BEE: It was a long time ago. *(Pause.)* We were different people then. *(Pause.)* We were children.

EM shuts her eyes. BEE looks out into the night.

BEE: Look, I saw one, look, a shooting star! At last I saw one.

Silence.

EM: A dying meteor.

EM doesn't open her eyes. Her lips are moving in prayer.

BEE: What are you doing? Em? Em?

EM opens her eyes.

EM: 'Be kind to little animals or they will bite you. You must not be seen dead in mauve. Do as I say and not as she does. Always change your knickers every day.' *(Silence.)* The lesson.

BEE: The lesson.

EM: And I remember when you fell over and broke your wrist. She wouldn't let me help you up. But I was there. She wouldn't let me.

BEE: Where did she go?

EM looks to the spot where CHRIS fell. BEE follows her gaze. She crosses to see better. Silence.

BEE: Oh fuck.

EM: Yeah. Fuck.

BEE: Oh shit.

Pause.

EM: What time is it?

BEE: Did she fall?

EM: What's the time?

BEE: Oh god.

EM: Bee? The time.

BEE: Oh my god.

EM takes hold of BEE's wrist and looks at her watch.

EM: Just gone two.

BEE: She fell?

EM: When the clocks go back.

BEE: Did she fall?

EM: No.

BEE: What then?

EM: I pushed her.

BEE: You pushed her?

Pause. BEE turns EM to face her.

EM: She wasn't a nice person, Bee.

Pause.

BEE: You pushed her.

Set back to:

BEE turns EM to face her.

EM: She wasn't a nice person, Bee.

Pause.

BEE: You pushed her.

They repeat the exchange three times. Silence.

BEE: What's that in your hand?

EM looks down and studies the remote. Then points it at the music centre. 'There's been a murder in the red barn' comes on. They listen for a few bars, then EM turns it off.

They both look over the edge and remain transfixed by the body of CHRIS.

BEE: Em.

EM: What?

BEE: I just wanted to say

EM: What?

Pause.

BEE: /You're my best friend.

EM: You're my best friend, Bee.

BEE: Jinx.

They laugh and make a sign which is only comprehensible to them.

EM turns the tape on again with the remote. Another Tom Waits number, raunchy, loud, and difficult not to dance to.

EM's foot starts tapping to the music. BEE begins to move. Limb by limb, the music gets to them until they both find themselves dancing.

Soon, BEE is dancing wildly, rhythmically, a whirling dervish.

BEE: Who says I can't dance?

EM: Of course you can dance.

BEE: I fucking *can* dance I can I can I can dance.

She swirls and stamps around the stage, shouting and laughing.

EM dances across to the table, jumps up onto it, pours herself a glass of wine and starts to drink.

BEE notices. She jumps up onto the table and does the same. They toast each other's glass and continue to dance upon the table.

THE END.

www.ingramcontent.com/pod-product-compliance
Ingram Content Group UK Ltd.
Pitfield, Milton Keynes, MK11 3LW, UK
UKHW020729280225
455688UK00012B/570

9 781849 430609